We enter the

Piet Nieuwland

Acknowledgements

Some of these poems have appeared in the following publications and exhibitions:

Otoliths, NZ Given Words, Fast Fibres Poetry, Poetry New Zealand Yearbook, A Fine Line, Verse of Silence, Taj Mahal Review, Verdant, Love In The Time Of Covid, Erothanatos, The Fringe of Heaven, This Twilight Menagerie and Parihaka & Manaia

Thanks to the Northland poetry community, ONEONESIX and Lisa

Contents

Meeting Again

With our imaginary eyes

the balance of the world tilts

We take glances from each other

spilling in to the spring wind

that opens windows to a lightness of being

and give glances to each other

with pieces of the past that inhabit

the what is happening

With eyes on the tips of our fingers

I feel you breathing

Your shoulder sinks into the quiet foam

olive skin oblivious to the gentle flood of shadows

that pours from doorways

to the map of living

Change our lives

Candelabra flicker from every surface

there's no place that doesn't see you

you must change your life

Yellow wash of silk coils the skiff

loaded with starlight, strand of cloud for a sail

a fabric death has woven around you

the cloth life wove into you

counting almonds, the dissolving

contours of forests, coasts, deserts and icebergs

Bodies, corpses, drawn by gravity to the earth

where does the soul go then?

no escape, to the next body and then…

we must redraw the map of things

re-imagine ontology's

We must change our lives

Greed is out of control

The fires blaze in parabola breathing

the adventurous wind, its yellow borders on

the ultramarine calligraphy of souls

the knife blade of vague shadow

To be myself living in the wind

and in the cloud where

anything may come

from a direction we least expect it

when we are least prepared,

to pause tenderly

sleep in the grass

to visit the planets docile leopards

and tend flocks of green and white elephants

where red swans with violet eyes ply

the ribbons of the lost landscapes

Of Waikato river deltas

Seeing, the systematic of

The systematic of seeing on an afternoon dense like a tangle of rags

with mirrors covered from presumptions of death

the slow nocturnal steps of darkness lead us to the chocolate coffee

aromas of dawn

when we compose in soft luxuriant promises, line by line, on the

eloquence of rain

of life passing from night into mirrors, of things pretty much

working out

on a weekend of buses and Waiheke ferries

a newborn grandchild, the daughter smiling happy proud the

husband busy tired

photographs of ancestors, whose names and facial features

some of us inherit

a reflective walk at the beach, the ocean unusually tranquil, calm

here we are, by the vertical law of gravity

by horizontal laws of relationship and community

splashed whirlpools of illusion

the melancholy beauty of bones

In a disturbed south west flow with embedded fronts

We make love with lost eyes inhabiting the velocity of time

and enter history at midnight silently

spiders ballooning on parachutes of silk

glide by on the earth's electric fields

beside the lotus of the blue divine I call you with voices and grins

with glances and apples, with smiles and maple syrup

with presences, pancakes and open ears

with replies, mysteries and waterfalls

chronology and assistance

with the brilliance of a lemon

the accent behind your laughter

in the huge blue night full of flickering eyes

our voices flare in the call and response

angel's wings, linen sheets of the nights canopy

ride the liberation of air in the mirrors of history

fine feathered plumes burst from evening stars

we mourn the clouds of the sea

A train is in our living room

Jumbo jet planes land in the bedroom

cars stream down the hallway, cars occupy the lounge

trucks are using the bathroom there is a supertanker on the toilet

flaming tapers and steel glass towers

home to strange polyhedral neurosis

compared to the undisputable beauty of the swan

      its complete and balanced mythology

as it passes over allegorical hills beyond reach

      to the bow wave in boreal inlets

      around milk trees laced with liana

as it passes in the uncertain scattered sunlight ice

is melting, still melting with the speed of memory

      with the wind full in our face

      the star is still only a guide

and the ice is melting, still melting

in the downpours of afternoons

four decades long over exponential centuries

in drips n drops

This house

The house breathes

Curtains still, tickle

A door wheezes open

Cracks in the floor pause dust

Windows are generous in their generosity

The light bulbs never know secrets hidden

In the stairway cupboard darkness

Nor of people in newspapers under the hallway carpet

Or the circus of microbes

A child here left toys in the garden

Pieces of dolls

Their shadows

Our future is not a dream

The infinity of time cascades, a hot summer wind dissolves

through the day, each continuous moment, gathers with it

it's becoming

The pattern of sky thickens in the International System

whenever the heart stops a beat, our future is not a dream

summer unties the knot of legs that now spread

on the island of black jacks and red queens driven

by the insistent sweetness of matching and pairing

the ancestral clasp of bonds over food at tables like these

op-shop porcelain, homegrown potatoes, beans spinach beetroot

herbs and garlic infusing olive oil from a nearby grove, local

cheese and a little wine, freshly baked bread in conversations

about chickens gone clucky the unfolding narrative of books

or website news updates the weather

To plant some childhood in the taste of soil

Under a sky crowded with stars that press the horizon into shape

beside the peacock blue sea, its windy personality,

 its elusive nationality

we remember our hands, the wash through a flotilla of orchids

the silent language of her breathing skin

clay mixed in a monsoon-sum

thin black netting tangles

in the abandoned afternoon

memories fall from clouds

weaving the threads of tears

a river of promises falls from your hair

from your mouth of edible substances

the rose of an unfurled kiss

In this religion of gardens

Flax blazes blue up the valley

willows stream away with

a scatter of magpies fragment across the hills

waves of cloud nibble at wet stars

and anything is possible in the orchard now

on the shallow sunny slopes in the fertile

wet earth more or less equidistant

from the apples, apricot, and grapefruit

we open a hole then fill it with compost. Here

now stands a pear tree, triple grafted to make

what it will of the earthen strata, its part

of the process from the south

west corner wind empties the stillness

secret mechanisms of spring

show through.

The air in spring

A marination of opals and laughter's of rubies

night and the water washed, shake themselves free

the day bears oranges

when fathers meet with grandfathers

at well-tended vegetable plots

turn the compost out for the cotyledons burst

kiss of tendrils, adventures of hungry roots

For hungry children and grandchildren

to feel in their hands, the damp chocolate weight of humus

potatoes glowing like eggs

pods of beans laden on tepees

the carrots hidden plunge

solar systems of tomatoes, aubergines, zucchini

ancient murmuring sounds of peach trees in blossom

the air thick with foaming ecologies

chloroplasts ecstatic

Daylights liquid murmur

Daylights liquid murmur on the page of waters

wind, full of memories

river with no other expectation

than the sea

In autumns distant style

embers of syllables

in avalanches of foliage

Words graze my lips

in the incendiary wind

moments sparkle

onto prows

of embroidered stars

Into the fertile river

strewn with leaves

a soluble half-moon melts

Under a molecular sky

The lunar outline of the bell

an iconic curve that sparks fires of syllables

a distillation of sacred rivers

between the matters of ritual and habit

necessary in the passage of a day

the crisp sweet aroma of orange honey

on fresh toasted rye bread with a guerrilla expresso

in sunshine, a scatter of grains for the Orpington's,

an inter-dental brush on teeth then look to the distance

haze or inventive shapes of wind

that gulls and harriers patrol

inspect embedded puriri knots and peach

their binding net and so it goes

options of compost beds of potatoes

spinach beans tomatoes and zucchini

this space fills occupied

by the regenerating labyrinth of process

and blossoming system

Remember the numbering of clouds

Not in snow, nor ice but warm mists

Her eyes incandescent stars

A handful of words

Scribbled on ribbons of language woven

An unveiling of letters

On drying cotton sheets

A new alphabet of signs

Of fluid sounds

A miracle of hours unfolding

Sweet ellipses, a solar circle

Actions of electrons reaching

Beyond their orbit

On Ruawai Wairua

The sky is my confidante

as we note oscillations of cloud geometry

where the silty fresh Northern Wairoa River meets

flows over salty clean Kaipara Harbor incoming tidal stream

zero meters above sea level,

Ruawai 2 meters below sea level at high tide

The two are inseparable at that hard-to-see-moment when

the tide turns around at the wharf where

campervans arrive, attend to picnics, ablutions and depart

though a town that retains its kauri bones of buildings,

painted in mirror image on the Long Flat Bacon Company

mural of 1928 at a State Highway 12 bend the church

now an op-shop, new pizza parlor with recycled red

stools, dairy factory become kumara warehouse

para-olympian hand cyclist training with makers of boat

mooring buoys, kind of busy

and like Holland, stop-banks, dykes, ditches, canals,

floodgates and pumps if necessary according to the Council

notice climate change leads to sufficient sea-level rise

greasy mud gleam on channel bank follows the falling tide

returning fishermen with quartets of snapper haul boats up

the slippery ramp, seagulls scan for fish scraps from wharf

piles with long shadows over the Wairoa River mouth

its catchment venation half of Northland Region

As the sun lands on the edge of the world

like an infinite rose about to shatter

a slow perfectly silent explosion

La Luna in full blossom

Kaipara time and time again

I

We would always take the long road home

the back road, windy, gravelly, dusty

with lonely farmhouses nestled amongst fruit trees

and the shelter of huge macrocarpa

a shearing shed beside a row of gnarled pines

the quiet back road with rowdy mobs of sheep

II

Returning to the sparkling waters twisting and turning

with beautiful daughters floating downstream

on Kaipara time

in Kaipara time

III

At Whakapirau the old dairy factory

on the wharf is being restored

as a boat club, restaurant or just a bach!

on a water tank a Sam hunt poem, a muddy inlet

across to Pahi, busy

a foreshore rubbish fire flares

IV

Paparoa Market is a Salt River

quartet with organic cabbages, woven breads,

heritage apple trees, eggs free range

local oysters' salty plump fresh slurp yum

V

Below slumped low cliffs

along the shallow clay-stone beach

harakeke flexes in the wind

a hangi pit marks a summer feast

across at Karakanui Point

ghosts of rich coastal forest

now denuded hills of urea green

VI

A classic long low Logan launch

ambles off to a favourite fishing spot

calm in the violet dusk

a new Kaipara punt named

'Back to the Future' waits

another spin down the river

on   long   slow   wing   beats

VII

The lung of harbour expels

drains another oceanic breath

and a breeze blows ice-cream cone clouds of the day

away

VIII

Girls on thick hawser swings arc

across the silt laden river

screams of glee

it's another Kewpie Two

day to day and a kotare call

Arrangements

In parallel, antenna of polynomial threads

braided filaments connect to what we are in the immoral

afternoon at the circular nuptial stone drenched with spores

the cottons damp with sweat spilled on by trillions

of imaginary numbers that count Vedic fibers in the heat

when the wave swipes across from Terra Australis, we slowly

melt into pools, meeting in the details, minute

Arrangements and re

Alignments

momentary nervous intimacies of breath

kiss on cheek a meeting of eyes for longer then

and then across aquamarine symmetries and lush

verdant rotations of rain flow through

finances and fiancés and always children

there somewhere

+ new-borns too

A latent catapult

On gravel terrace

Grave mounds fill

With sorrow, sorrow

Mountains disappear

Behind the sky

Trembling shadows

Laden with lament

The gate opens

Falcons on wing

Endless rivers

Come drumming in

Through autumn golden

Bright orb on dark sea

Each moment a pounamu

Memory, our hearts now

Showers of point centered scintilla

A-saalam ahi koum

"Assalaam alaykum"

Beside the orchid pavilion

Flowers bloom like madness in the spring

tall bamboo foliage curves

and curves on river transparent quiet

as silk meandering lantern light skiffs sail into harbour mouth

Green vines braid to high forest

as clouds scatter into brocade

Warm air quickens with yellow birds

A peach moon flies across the vivid sky

Temple of Teeming Fragrance jade pendants tinkle in wind

our tears swell together, we weep

dark water flows through flower beds

candles glow in solemn mist

river of stars a web of tears

On a black sign

Ragged gardens choked

with fruit trees vegetables and vines

a parquet of heaps and piles

transfigurations of strange

yet familiar beauty turning

amongst a sequence of signs

a diagram of interference

in the electrical wind, in the sky

the nothing but sky spiraling

volumes from Mare Imbrium

mask the cavernous grief

a slow exploding silence of death

time shrinking faster

than the speed of light

into a vertical chaos

Of exponentials

[like this]

In the shallow banks of time, a strangers memory

A velvety atlas, slowly, lovingly, fine sheets of tissue peel back

Without knowing what to say

Like seeds in the loam of a flowerbed

You dream of a bride in red

You return to the womb of your mother

Wings of your nostrils fold

Sobbing, the wind flies off

The transparent day

Is vulnerable, affectionate

As if after a morning of lovemaking

At on edge of incrementally rising waters, you go

With the salt, your shadow

Breaking away from your legs

At a river unknown to anyone

Kites scribe verbs in the sky / for the empires of angels

The elastic water / a distant terrain of news cut

From an infinite bolt / of fabric

The future uncovers / in the sound of mirrors

An imaginary hour

Your skin asleep / woken by kisses

Your triangular garden blossoms / in colours of memory

At the accurate temperature

A mellifluous fecundity / in dark scintillations of soil

The infinite literature of hips

A fiesta of gradual pressures

A granulation of stars / burst at the weight

Of hair

At the pipiwharauroa call

A rumour of motion

on a nameless black river

In the silence of leaf fall

with tuna in the water of dreams

Living continues and spring blooms

Unwinding a tree of music

a sudden silence of black swans

a-flight across the estuary

She with a basket-full of black plums

falling into distances

deciding where trees should be planted

all-over

again

Between nocturnal pools

In the morning I am clouds, in the evening I am rains

Time is eclipsed beyond the raga-sphere

in the magnitude of bright hours

that encapsulates the cool solitude of dawn

A meditation on self-acceptance

follows a shadowy symmetry of circles

that move in the space creative forming

between stars and constellations

Between islands, continents and gardens

knotted cords stretched tied and tangled

spell medleys of twang tone pitch and cadence

We return to the oceanic pulse of conception

and break into each other

singing the song of songs

Drowning in a dazzle of flowers

a precariat of petals

the colour of memory

The imaginary hour

Stars granulate on sheets of silica

The skin of your body asleep

woken by kisses to the triangular garden

it blossoms in colours of memory

at the accurate temperature

a mellifluous fecundity

in a dark scintillation of soil

the infinite literatures of your hips

a fiesta of gradual pressures

Stars burst at the weight

of your hair

With a line escaping

So the coast comes to light out of milky shadows

With a line escaping from

Rakaumangamanga to Purerua, beyond

in a now flood of decades marking me

as of this place / is my place / is us here

a film filling narrative of rhythm and blood

the birth and adolescence of ultra-cool and groovy

enthused and distracted by soft lunar tissues

in a chaos of lightning, webs of cyclonic rain, sky woven like rags

arguing with the world in subversions, dissent, undercurrents

asking what are you prepared to give up or curtail or change

in our cultures of creativity, in the

who we are of the day, in the

open generosity and kindness, in the

fun of variety, in the friends forming, in the

you are us with we are you

that the planet will be a much better place for everything

And everyone

With Veronica Channel

From the moon soaked pulpy flesh of night

all that now exists is like the surface of waters

on the scattered islands of marama

with tui song pure as water drops falling

onto the sand dunes of her hips

we embrace like branches of trees/ in fragile blossom

in tears from the blood of the earth

A dawn wind skims the river mirror

the angled prow of waka suspended on opalescence

ecotonal forest breathes out an aroma complex of night

from a hilltop room a piano with friends rides the ocean of cloud

in surging skeins it weaves / a cultural cartography

on the flight of birds /

the lament of black cockatoo and white heron

flows from the keys / from falling fingers that weep

The peninsula post

For now all is quiet on the Waitangi front.

Below Rakaumangamanga cascades of bays melt in the summer sun.
From giant fig shade, varieties of human experience and ultra-violet
exposure emerge and dissolve into shimmering heat on
Oneroa/Long beach.

A trilogy titled Bay Belle, Waitere Blue and Happy Ferry cross and
criss from Paihia to here and back and back again here to
Kororareka. The R Tucker Thompson, a gaff rigged schooner
under full sail cruises out on another afternoon from the Hell Hole
of the Pacific. Now it's a goulash of tourist accents and barely
gravid honeymooners holding hands, holding conversation, holding
berry blossoms of ice creams from the devilishly devilish parlour.

A duo in kayaks paddles over to that quiet beach below those cliffs.
Outside the Duke, still refreshing rascals and reprobates since 1827
we toast deliciously (again) on the late afternoon gravel beach
splashing into it, in to the pale silvery green, looking across to
Waitangi at 2021 (again).

Through spreaders of yacht masts, flag poles, ship yardarms and
gull wings our bodies stretch out reptilian under the pohutukawa

grey. On another day (again) luckier than we care to imagine, we watch the water through the trees. The waves carry the full moon through the branches, a tuna glances up

Mander Park afternoon

Girl on a swing swing high

        Girl on a swing swing fly

                Girl on a slide slide by

      Girl on a slide slip slide hi ya

                    Girl on a see boy on a saw

        Girl on a see saw with a boy

      Girl on a saw seen with a boy

Boy seen with a girl on a see saw

Mum with a baby

Grandad with a pram

Auntie with a stroller

Uncle with a kid's dad, a man

Mum with a baby, a dog

Grandad with a pram and a turban

Auntie with a stroller and boy with a bike

Uncle with a girl on a red trike

Play world

In the garden of mazed pathways we walk ride climb

play skip hop and jump

in and around boulders caves and rock walls

on and around stairways paths and alleyways

over frames down slides along narrow beams over bridges swinging

around trees being primate up trees high into trees

along the cantilevered branches of trees overhanging

fresh deep clean swimming holes

dropping with a bomb of splashes

in the maze drifting down stream in the cool kowhai shade

where tui gargle and clap joining shrieks screams and laughter

that bubbles out of the thrill of gravity and flow motion

The spin the whirl

Over worn surfaces

In the night wind

  With an amazing frequency

      Looks like this

Fertile as the gardens of your forefathers

Conversations on sophisticated issues

    Being immersed in the concerns

   Of the world and

Of things that need not be mentioned

On a terrestrial voyage

    Through the hearts geography

      Hour upon hour joined

      In their sequences

Over the worn surfaces of light

     How they keep happening

       Like freight trains on tracks to Otiria

Sounding the trajectory of rails

Over the water, night

And the river

The garment of an uproar

The garment of an uproar of birds over a deep blue malachite ocean

A rustle of human leaves wanders under the light clouds canopy

The fresh wound of a voice from a mother's blood

Weaves words like the body of an infant

Night gathers unfocussed stars brushed by lips of radiance

And splashes moonlight upon indigo forests of shadow

Wearing a yellow shirt and glance back to those evenings when

The fires of youth burned silence broken by alloys of static tattered

Spindling on riddles that linger in celebration of a whole life long

I recognise the latitude where I was born in the fluid dark

 of early morning

I recognise the longitude where the river changes polarity

On the thin edges of things in my life

On a whim provoked by a long lasting flood plain

where coastal silt presses

Closer to a random point on an island known by its trembles

A handful of freckles melted down into a secret freedom

To be unlike all the rest

To be pop or not to bebop

The pregnant moon glides thick, fleshy, in awe

of the waters invisible geography

of magically clear shorelines diving deep

of the skies shimmery smoulder

of the immense ultramarine amphitheatre of silence

of the labyrinthine bounty of submarine forests

of light stretched over the ocean, mirror upon mirror upon mirror

of the Whakaari phreatic power

of the plumage of ash black exploding

Supersonic invisible instants

Of before and after

The warm yellow cadmium yellow sulphurous yellow straw yellow

serum yellow that leaks

from summer burning at both ends

skinny dipping with nano-plastic and phytoplankton

your life a sonnet that unfurls in a day

as I fall from myself

into another self

in a dream of ash that floats past cliffs

in a dive that ends

as evenings bloodshot sun ignites in our hands

momentarily oblivious

to the parameters of a Berkeley Madonna tetra-pak

of gigaflops of hydro-data

joined in mutual liquefaction

Filaments of the universe

In frantic cloud flow

the water moves

the water is moving

the water is aqua-clinal-aqua-form-flow hydro-logically

hydrometric in spooled liquid threads and splash

of monsoon timpani tentacles of shadow

each drop recognising itself

in other drops

in others flooding

from the cloud house

where it was raining inside each window

it was raining where the sky ended

it is raining inside us

it was raining at Tangihua

and it is raining at Tangowahine

and it was raining in the delicate friendship of trees

in drops, in sweet disorders of summer frisson

Soaking your dress of champagne

With unspoken questions

With unspoken questions / on bioluminescent algae

Viridescent infinities / emerald harmonics

We embraced the swollen arch of dawn / its twisted silken chords

Over archipelagos of white winged yachts /

on a deep aquamarine gauze

On course to hidden magic bays / dialects of landscapes

Fecundities of spirit / fertile subversions

Dancing tarantellas of coastal dunes

Vivid cadenza in the diluvial light

As when we love / these wounded black mountains

As when we follow / the edge of tidal water / through salt flats

From this hill / feeling an uneasy peace

When the sun lifts / out of the ocean

The houses / sown loosely / amongst totara groves

All huddle and flex / in tentacles / of the hot wind

We enter the

We enter the same river as shadows / dissolving black mosaics

put calculations aside / and examine our selves

amongst jumbled ice floes/ in the polar night

with waves re-naming the beaches

in communions / on a hundred thousand altars of oak and stone

at deserts of windmills / and turbines of light

with Panthalassa crying / eternities of hot tears

at our theatrical spectacle / of frantic dance

chants of masks banners and flags

of feathers, leaves and painted faces

building the momentum / of unheard-of terms

in galloping downpours of hyper-typhoons

Under a sky full of eyes

In the breathe that passes through the palace of light

with a diffuse magma of words

above the river / over the river / on the river / in the flow

insignia of instants cart-wheel like covid cluster scatters

no doubt unaware of the gravitational constant

let alone a global media profile that money couldn't buy

over melancholy landscapes of collapsing futures

littered with paradigms of closed theorems

where belief in god is considered a sign of weakness

we rehearse our understanding of freedom with responsibility

reinventing the fabric of our patterns of doing stuff

enmeshed in the laws of biology

crossing the boundaries of history and memory

under a sky full of eyes

with organo-phonics on this boney ridge

where with patience and flags we create a territory of new sentences

swallows going like windborne rumours

Vulnerable

With morning stars shimmering in night blue filigree

A pianissimo of valley fog in slumber

The dew of day break sings songs without words

Beside the railway track at Mangapai station

A clear stream runs over grassy moss and stone

As the tidal river makes its move through mangrove margins

She arrived in the elementary hour anorexic as a photograph

In the microscopic light, with eyes of rouge

Cheekbones vivid as shadows

We did not know if she was infected, there were no symptoms

No coughing or sneezes, no headaches

Asking us to explore the illusion of individual freedom

And infinite possibilities

With night unfolding its dark cloak

And the blade of a new moon rising

We are all afraid of the same thing at the same time

The social amplification of risk

Our vulnerability

The luminous plasma

In the ripening days

Beneath the suns luminous plasma

We walk on the shadows of gum trees

Where tui call and magpies craw

Clouds ferment over the dark bladed Maungatapere cone

A chorus of leaves merge into the chemical process of the day

The afternoon sky stretched thin as a clinical sheen

Of cellophane, the coast ignites in a surf-line sea dazzle

I spread myself thin

I spread myself thin like sunscreen across the colours of the day

a magnetic field attracting languages of light and landscape

of people and particles

absorbed by the thick green of those flame trees at this park

immersed into the mercurial blue of the dancing wide river

taken by the sand filtering through my hands and hair

as it pours over me

shattered by the immense sky blown to beyond

by star bright and the turbid moon

fixated by the isotopes and emulsions of people,

the crystallography of their eyes,

and the curvatures of their greeting accents

in the morning calm

Hokianga singularities

The body a sensory field / laid out in the morning dew

upon the eyes and chest / tiny mandala of petals and leaves

fingers bound by coloured ribbons of time

a voice escaping in a cadence of verbs

across spilling orange textures of Kahakaharoa sand

across singularities / tidal current vectors / the living breath,

the west wind accumulating cumulus

translations of restless imaginations / sparked by flits of swallows

or a phrase from a book whose pages / open today with as much

to say about this as we want them too, or not /

like 'the seething almost Indian heat' not of temperature

but chilli powder with the chain that passes through my back /

 pulling taut upwards against the gravity of this transient body /

whose bones now feel more prominent

tight-rope walking on a line of thought / zone of experience

cloud of perception / fluid array / like swallowing

a glass of fresh cool water and you return / ripe as a kiss

In pohutukawa

Arte Povera: 'The vertigo of igloos and fruits, the flight of stones on the blue horizon, the melting of ice and crazy colour' Germano Celant 1985

In the garden of sky / stars broadcast their flirtations

with luminous colour shifts

An incense of ocean curls off / the dark horizontal stretched

at both ends

From here to there / this place to that, and those,

and many more beyond

Flotillas of flowering cleavages / as invisible mermoids

and mermaids ride

Pairs of bejewelled silver prows / hearts reflecting

in the shimmering breeze

Summer freshness springs again / living / with so much living

In and around the coastal current vectors / at Awarua Rock

Springs again / from dripping peaches and capsicum globes /

the crunch

Of bright verdure, scarlet and succulent oranges / dribbled sticky

sweet / rock melon

And long slow curves of soft sand / recline

a seduction in pohutukawa

Shade and surround sound surf / surrenders to temperature

As a tree branch

At Puweto Valley Aorangi Island / I am a twisted branch of *Nestegis apetala* / a coastal maire tree / end of a limb that began / before we knew it / beneath the southern sun / that scans a mazarine Moana oceania / amongst a pohutukawa tawapou canopy / casting shadows that evaporate over the lens of the day / leaf buds articulating the momentary thoughts of clouds / we come from the stars / we were the land before we were people / dancing a Pacific drum song / playing burning violins / grand pianos overcome by surf / and in the singing mirror of night / a calabash of stars flung over

Jewel points

A silicon moon waxes / as the night train rumbles south

we bathe in a luminous glow /

soft murmurs of shadows fall in tranquility

Tangihua peaks razor across the endless sky

ragged headlands dressed in a fatal calligraphy

the flame of dawn claws like an arrhythmic heartbeat

morning parakeets shriek and blaze and dazzle

tilting harriers cut ever widening arcs

black clouds blossom

In lockdown love

The pages of the sky open in one sector of the universe

With wings that sail on the sensuality of time

In the maze of light and air

Over the we of us, the us of us, the us of the earth

The earth that is us, the we

In our own ways of living

In the sublime transience

With today never being the same again

Of doing simple things we like and need to

That makes the day turn over into night again

Being quite satisfied with apples harvested

Trees pruned, compost spread, seeds germinating

Dishes and clothes washed, flat breads made

A sociable wave to passing neighbours

And the aroma of stir-fry vegetables curling through

The cottage with our hearts burning

On a beam that goes through the ionosphere

On Egretta sacra in descent

On the descent of Pacific reef herons

from a magnolia of night along their endless

curves of desire, its gossamer threads

The electric ocean charges / discharges as a wild north-eastern

sea collides in foam of argument over Mangawhai Heads

dune cliff harbour mouth rocky reef tidal current vector confluence

On the sheltered side, young pied shags in pohutukawa roost

drop their bright white splashes onto Pseudopanax below

On the open coast side Taranga incises the wind

Te Whara headland lies long brooding distant

and the low shoulders of Marotere Islands huddle

these sanctuaries all blazing natural profusion

bird song streams off in visible swirls of braided chords

At the kinetic confluence

kite surfers dance on pulsing waves of air

on lookers in awe of the aerial acrobatics

The fine sands trap easily in our eyes bringing tears

so we turn, walk back, heads bowed in the maelstrom

Back at the holiday park we arrange a meal in the camp cookhouse,

simple pasta and vegetables

despite the mid-winter there are people here to chat with

locals who home-school their children in lockdown

In the wind there's blood,

it shifts, sorts, sifts, re-sorts the flesh of the world

layers of surfaces buried beneath are opened up

torn, cut, into skin, in the forest of gone

fall flowers of light, ambitious clouds in torment

Weather Report

The wheel turns

From a whispering silky sea / weightless turquoise sky

To ribbons of air unwinding skeins of linguistics

Of a leaden sky / grey metallic green ocean

Torn surf flecked with stretched foams and pale blues

Bream Bay coastal current vectors twist and roll

On this periphery of ragged headlands and islands

The horizon not a line but a zone of incrementally

Rising undulations driven in from Antarctic ice shelf melt

Arctic melt, glacier melt, permafrost melt, thermal expansion

Mesmerizing in their fresh salt laden intrigues

That leaves on the high tide flotsam / jetlag line

A pig (sow), bloated, on a spit (sand)

Bunch of bananas (lady finger) edible

Plastic star jump toy (green)

Fragments of memory (happy) and distressed

The swells find they have no-where else to go

Fall into a jumble of meter and structure

Cultural theories of life/art as object / practice / process

Also described as sea level rise crisis panic

Hypothesis

Oh greetings from the upper arms / closed fists

the front door is a place made for occasions / in ridge crest clouds

with a green wind / in eyes of sapphire green

a karoro whanau wheels geodesic equations into an easterly storm

we hunker down into bowls of thick porridge

with home-grown apples

as a season of sneezing begins / and hill-slopes weep

soft terrorisms of sports field lights flood the sky volcanic

floating co-ordinates of the age / a wild cacophony of presence

estuarine alveoli clog with plastic mucus drowned in Covid plasma

we live in constraints of dynamic collapsologies

series of good intentions displayed on liquid crystals

To the people we love.

Inhabiting pages

Inhabiting pages of hours in kaleidoscopes of time

in days that dissolve into cartwheels

Trusting, in the wide air breathing in, breathing out

trusting in cleaned hands, washed again, and again

In the outlook of green hills greener, green, trees greener

In the blue sky music

in the confinement of just our bodies on short walks

In the marginal places we imagine in our minds eyes

in the daily WHO updates of exponentially

Escalating catastrophes of bodies piled high

of bodies delivered in refrigerated trucks

of bodies buried en-mass in bulldozed trenches

Of shrinking back into the small safe place curled

up in bed, deep under cover, next to you

Enjoying the fresh olfactory memories of spiced apple

pie we've just made, the shared roles

You rolling the dough, me chopping apples

into an alchemy, carnal as the resonant wind

News from nowhere

When the vigorous night bleeds with abundant plums

we speak the language of clematis, blossoming opals

your body takes the shape of my hands, the earth

is blue like an orange with a necklace of wings

the black flag of the sky is sown with stars woven in muka flax

we are all African in the dancing of water of the curved shore

and the breathing mountains, and the wondrous fruits of the earth

- (like/with/as) pomegranates on fire
- nectarine breasts dressed with silk
- mathematical nights of avocado
- flavors of long distance phone calls
- voices un-quarantined in mahogany jungle chants
- a dance of liquid hieroglyphics
- scents of hair in oceanic starfish
- silvery bonito fibril flash
- submarine explosions of kisses
- crescendos of dark weeping
- puriri trees cloaked in black lightning
- torrential cacophonies
- hyperactive frontal systems
- shattered mirrors of our selves
- dissolving

We ride through forests of stone

We ride through forests of stone on horses with scarlet hooves
bought online from Arab traders in Tabriz and are joined by knights
wearing full suits of armour made of chocolate and marzipan

Arriving at a neoliberal arts auction in the Wynyard Quarter the
Fijian whale tooth necklace rattles ominously as bidding starts and a
cabal of hopeless bankers begin mumbling to each other

At a nearby outdoor GO tournament, a frowning competitor
wearing a full bottomed periwig describes his technicolour dreams
where the pieces turn into hermaphroditic beetles that eat
themselves

On old woman still dressed in her wedding gown and living in a
disused oil tank overlooking the square receives a happy meal
delivered by a giant introducing himself as Svante Arrhenius

After being dissolved in enzymes from the second salivary glands
and swig of contreau, the snack of oysters and tamarind chutney
became bright blue as it travelled down the metastisizing esophagus

She was also disturbed by a new mutation of a pungent yellowish
fungus spreading through her skin from each armpit in painful welts
accompanied by rapid micro-spasms in her eyes and dry retching

Return to another green world

We are everyone's words

amongst the branches of night

inhabiting the infinite substance of marmalade and blood

On a Brazilian five string double bass the poem

 is a constellation of plasma

asserting the challenge, freedom is the choice of necessity

as we watch in awe,

at the forests unsuspected capacity for tenderness

As when they wait beside cottage gardens fertilized

by flocks of crystalline parrot s and communes of bees

for the nearby river

night is a cloak in the hours of ringing bells and minutes of silence

In the sobbing distance, very far away

hallucinated people flock like birds in the parabolic trees of nightfall

women pray tears, hands telling the drops

The mask is a face is the mirror is the red moon

in the fluid music of early morning mist is moving

to describe the world, to say so, to say so

In the space of a day

reflections telescope me into the world

of peaches and oranges,

that spill from the opened gloves of the earth

Nestled in hollows of the bride

they ask, what is it for the dead to remember the living

when the best shroud for the dead, is a starlit night

Along sub-cutaneous geometries

Along sub-cutaneous geometries of the harbour edge

and beyond to the sea, a soprano-like allegory of enormous

and delicate silences

sculptured with gravitational folds

the clouds are tangled echoes and liquid

gamelan rills over Takahiwai

followed, by a great internal heat-wave stretched over the horizon

I stand in the distance looking at us

rain falls upon mossy translucent viridians underfoot

spaces of meaning close around fibrils of beginning

air heavy, nervous with colours of listening

You remember an event corresponding to me forgetting a name

recalling a face

what would this be if we were our children?

At the grove

In the grove of luminary beings / happy in the patterns of trees

canopies surprise us / with their lush foliage of emerald stars

amongst silken tents of wind /

the first trembling gossamer on the silvery mirror

the landscape of your iris dissolves /

into subtle glints of kapowairua

in this sanctum of luxuriant shade / cool damp and ferny silence

the eyes of every creature gaze / on a vault of the past

clouds ferment on the Parihaka skyline

tanekaha sway to the cries of children

In the eclipse

in the eclipse of haze over Parihaka

uncertainly maps layers of liquid topographies

behind you

     evening is Aotearoan

       it slips its dark arms

         around the knots of distance

like the way people move through us

     in the moments of a day

       in the moments of moments

        that drip from leaves

I no longer pretend

     each gesture meaningless

that there is no memory held in the nikau frond

         nor the plump red puriri berry

as it falls onto the mulched fabric of the soil

        the unfolding song of the land

Arrival and departures

Touched by light wavering across all that darkness

      music of atmospheres plays out in cirrus

            from the tangled mesh of sleep we are too late to be

                        anywhere else

on midnight the boat glides into the harbour

      masts of marina yachts swing in agreement

         convey adjectives of arrival

the weight of February lies on the land

      either side of the river the dead lie buried

            manawa pods drift out in the last of the tide

our breaths are lost in the obvious air

      from the underside/this side of the nights stars

      continental shapes of music uncover from buried strata

new requiems of plastic garbage from exposed waste dumps

         are reduced to small futures of invention

presents saturated with multiple pasts stretch out

      on intricate shorelines laden with sand, sky, light

      ocean salt

Puriri moth alights

Waipoua Forest blazes ecstatic in the midday sun

the tall ones, kahikatea on the alluvial flats

vivid green alchemies of ridgeline kauri

at this place of river valley peace

We are the land / poetry is a sacred site

water-birds alight / raupo fronds sway in the immortal winds

the river takes us in / whispering "come join with me"

I am pulled, fall, stumble in

Is this a life changing moment I ask

emerging from the dense fresh liquid / one of many I answer

A kahu tail fan brushes clouds like grey clay

on the blue field of sky

our breathe dances in the light of feathers

light dances on the leaves

leaves dance to songs of birds

These rivers remember / the sounds of children's voices

cascades of summer cicada / a deafening dawn chorus

tuna circling under shaded banks / puawhananga falls

and rata blooms

These rivers remember / how the forest feels on their banks

puriri moth flies free from surface

The spiral lattice

In the role of observer in a prestigious anti-gravity landscape a waterfall coaxes the atmosphere with singing clouds, offering no escape from our collective responsibility.

In a polyphonic tussle of language amongst the characters of a narrative, the linearity of our experience is remapped. Its multiple subjectivities created by prized specimens of scientia-feminae at the temperature of water.

In political climatology, the itineraries of perpetual motion and e-motion of fronts cross imaginary longitudes of wing beats and apertures, their instabilities at the rates of entropy.

Small squiggle-like entities are reduced to insignificance on the edgeless boundary of a vast planar territory where in the semiotics of petrified light the optics of their instincts dissolve into cinematic depths where nothing is reflected.

Feel, inside your hearts

inside your hearts, feel

the forest is society and we are the trees

in the intangibility of seasons when beans germinate

the beach carves deeply into orgasm

fills with gems, bright, young, splashing frolicking

in surf and sun shine asking what if?

people paused in inter-zonal states of what is really important

an instinctual mimicry of remote futures

darkness folds upon darkness

filling the notes of a thousand birds

with polysyllabic murmurings of Chinese, French, Maori, English

and Indian

and hieroglyphic isotopes of microbe communities

sculpted in concise vivid sequences

of cadmium pale yellow and deep red

ultramarine and cerulean blue with titanium white

with our glands exuding volatile hormones

forming new allegiances in gravitational transitions

When we go down to the waters

When we go down to the waters

      follow the ghost wind

            through the ghost trees

                To the tissues

                of dreams

The rattle of a new revolution shakes the shuttle of wind

Photons tumble in silent hot choreographies,

      angry incendiaries,

            showers of spark seeds

                taking root in the wet earth

In the hectic wind / with the morning star

      our voices the colour of watching

Rain at the edge of time / on the avian blade

      home shape-shifts

With currents and tricksters of history

      that surrounds it

Of this is to say *'in spite of my forebears they continued'*